THE GHOST IN THE MACHINE
AN UNTOLD CODE VERSE

Megami Rhymes

Copyright
© 2024 Megami Rhymes

All rights reserved. No part of this publication may be reproduced, distributed, or transmitted in any form or by any means, including photocopying, recording, or other electronic or mechanical methods, without the prior written permission of the author, except in the case of brief quotations embodied in critical reviews and certain other noncommercial uses permitted by copyright law.

For permission requests, write to the author at the email address below:
Email: quenzcraft@gmail.com
Visit the author's website at:
www.selfcraftlife.com

ISBN: 978-2-1550-3707-0

Publisher:Success Publications Sar
First Printing, 2024

DEDICATION

This book is dedicated to the unseen friends, the voices and spirits I've met in the expanse of digital realms—within the bounds of games where we have fought side by side, laughed, and shared secrets without ever sharing the same physical space. Your friendship transcends the limitations of geography and reality, proving that connections forged in virtual worlds are as real and profound as any made face-to-face.

And to poets, those brave souls who wield words like warriors, dance in the lines of verses and cast spells with stanzas. This is intended for those who strongly believe that poetry is alive, thriving, evolving, and crucial. Poetry reminds us that it can be a light in the darkness and a shadow in the midst of life, revealing truths that the heart knows but the mind sometimes fails to grasp.
May we find unity in our unseen bonds and beauty in our words, together.

FOREWORD

In today's digital age, the line between reality and virtuality blurs in ways once unimaginable. Love, once expressed through letters and whispers, now finds life in keystrokes and digital avatars. "The Ghost in the Machine: An Untold Verse Code" explores love and loss in this tech-driven world.

Each poem in this collection captures complex human emotions through powerful words and simple yet evocative illustrations. The verses invite readers into a world where the joy and sorrow of love are vividly portrayed, bridging the gap between digital and real-life experiences.

For young adults navigating digital relationships, poetry lovers, or anyone intrigued by the intersection of technology and emotion, this collection mirrors our times. It highlights the universality of love and loss, the quest for connection, and the resilience of the human heart.

As you read, may you see reflections of your own journeys, loves, and heartbreaks. Let these poems guide you through the digital landscapes of emotion, offering solace, understanding, and hope.

Welcome to "The Ghost in the Machine: An Untold Verse Code."

Megami Rhymes

TABLE OF CONTENTS

"The ghost that haunted my mind for almost three or four years, the precise timeline escaping my memory, remained with me unwelcomed. Will I ever be able to erase him from my thoughts completely? His existence in my mind endures, a daily meditation, as if he had carved a permanent home within the boundaries of my thoughts."

Section One:
Virtual Beginnings

THE GHOST IN THE MACHINE

In a universe where avatars twirl and quests
unite,
You logged into my existence, altering the script
of night.
This volume I pen—your tribute, your stage—
For the ghost within the circuits, the whisper of
the digital age.

You, the echo in the void of a vacated
chatroom's call,
The silent heartbeat shielded behind the screen's
tall wall.
Revealed to me love's reach, boundless and
deep,
Beyond the digital frontiers, where pixelated
emotions creep.

When you signed off, your essence lingered
like a soft light,
Etched in the circuits of my heart, through
endless day and night.
No update can erase the imprint you've
engraved,
No reboot dismisses, the memories we've
saved.

These lines, unposted, a whisper from realms
afar,
Notes from beyond the screen where our
endings are.
A ballad of "Game Over," where echoes still
play—
In the heart of a game where we once found
our way.

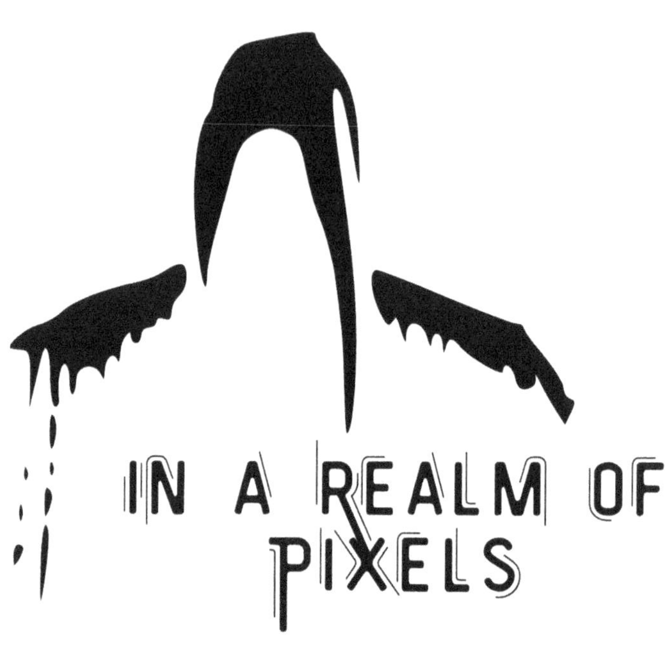

IN A REALM OF
PIXELS

A domain where fantasy and pixels blend,
We met as avatars with quests to lend.
A spark through screens, unseen yet brightly
lit,
Our digital footsteps synced, bit by bit.

You spoke in code, I laughed in emoticons,
Our world a tapestry of electric dawns.
Adventure called, across vast, virtual lands,
Our fates entwined by fate's unseen hands.

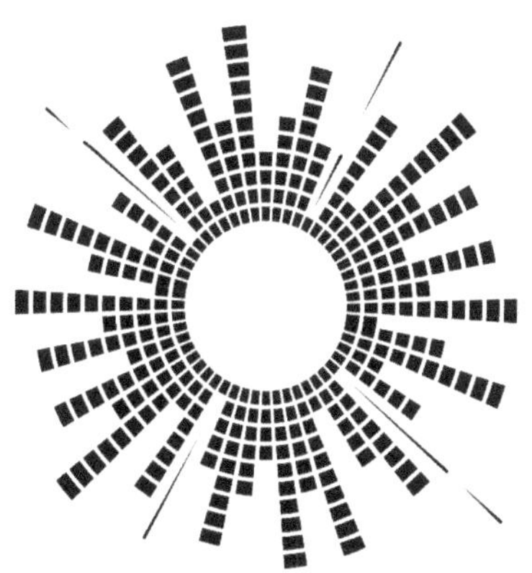

A Gamer's Dual Existence

In the glow of the screen, life unfolds,
A realm where the digital tightly holds.
Avatars roam in worlds so vast,
Each login a dive into a cast.

Living the game, where reality blurs,
Where warriors laugh, and history stirs.
Pixels ignite with every quest,
In landscapes where the soul can rest.

Swords clash and dragons soar,
Beyond the room, beyond the door.
Friendships forge in battles fierce,
Where pixels bleed and hearts can pierce.

The keyboard clicks are a rhythmic beat,
A gamer's heart, the echoing feat.
Life in the game, so vivid, so bright,
Colors that dazzle, banishing night.

Emotions ride on a coded wave,
Joy and sorrow, the brave and the brave.
Victories sweet and defeats that sting,
In the game, you're a peasant, a king.

Yet, when the screen dims, the room grows still,
The echoes of the game, against the will.
Life outside waits, a shadowed hue,
Yet inside, the game keeps renewing the view.

Living the game, a double-edged sword,
Balancing worlds, in accord.
Where do I end, where does it begin?
The game I play, the skin I'm in.

Connections in Code

Across the pixels, a laughter spreads,
In the space where digital threads
Weave a tapestry rich and vast,
Crafting friendships meant to last.

In chat rooms filled with vibrant hues,
We share our days, exchange our news.
Emojis fly, gifs dance and spin,
Each icon a grin, a virtual twin.

Virtual games, our common ground,
Where camaraderie is found.
Battles fought and races won,
Under the glow of a pixelated sun.

Movie nights through shared screens,
Discussing plots and favorite scenes.
Distance fades, closeness grows,
In streams of data, friendship flows.

Celebrations typed in caps,
Comfort found in virtual laps.
Support that spans the data streams,
In forums, feeds, and digital dreams.

Happy moments, not confined
By geography, just aligned
By hearts that beat in digital sync,
Without a pause, without a blink.

So here's to us, the online crew,
Finding joy in what we view.
Though miles apart, we're close at heart,
In the world where digital is an art.

AVATARS MEET
PIXELS IN CONFLICT

In the shadowed dominion of midnight raids,
Enemies first, in the game's harsh glades.
Clad in armor, sword and shield in hand,
We clashed on digital battlegrounds, unplanned.

Amidst the chaos of war's fierce embrace,
A spark ignited in that virtual space.
From foes to friends in a twist of fate,
Curiosity grew as animosity abate.

In the heat of conflict, our avatars found
A kinship formed on contested ground.
Strategies shared and secrets told,
In whispered chats, bold moves unfold.

Through the fog of war, our spirits danced,
Past barriers, where suspicion once glanced.
Not just warriors on scripted quests,
But souls connecting, amidst digital tests.

From battlegrounds to peaceful talks,
Our journey shifted on paradox walks.
Enemies in play, yet allies at heart,
A friendship forged—a new start.

THROUGH SCREENS

Through screens, our worlds collide and
mesh,
Digital whispers in a nightly refresh.
Words fly like sparks in virtual skies,
Hearts tentatively reach through digital eyes.

A message sent, a response delayed,
The subtle dance of characters displayed.
Each line a thread in a web we weave,
Invisible bridges built as we believe.

Smiles rendered in pixels bright,
Laughter echoing in the bandwidth's light.
Secrets typed with hesitant keys,
Unveiling souls in degrees.

Your humor a beacon, your kindness a sign,
Across vast networks, your spirit aligns.
Through screens, a friendship cautiously built,
On foundations of letters and emoticon quilts.

Yet in this realm where touch is a myth,
Feelings grow tangible, surprisingly swift.
A connection profound, defying the void,
In the quiet glow of screens enjoyed.

FIRST QUEST TOGETHER

Side by side in the
realm of lore,
A quest began, opening
a door.
Through enchanted
woods and dungeons
deep,
Together we'd leap
where shadows creep.

Pixels sparked beneath
our swift commands,
As our avatars faced
the darkened lands.
With every challenge
and monster slain,
Our bond grew strong,
a new domain.

A synergy found in the heat of battle,
Above the virtual war's constant rattle.
Strategies formed from whispered chat,
In moments where we stood, combatant stat.

Treasures sought in hidden chests,
Our teamwork put to the ultimate test.
Laughing through each failed attempt,
Finding rhythm in every step.

The quest's end found us victorious,
In shared joy, our spirits glorious.
Beyond mere players in a game played,
Comrades born from the alliance made.

Section Two:
Building Connections

BEYOND THE GAME

We started as allies in virtual quests,
Battling foes, passing each test.
Yet as the screen dimmed, our conversations
grew,
Beyond the game, to dreams and truths.

From avatars to voices over the line,
Our late-night talks, lost in time.
Sharing laughter, fears, hopes, and woes,
A friendship blossoming, tenderly it grows.

In this virtual realm, we found a door,
To something real, something more.
Not just pixels, but heartbeats sync,
Our lives intertwine in less than a blink.

You showed me worlds beyond the screen,
Places and stories yet unseen.
Through music shared and books discussed,
In each other, we found trust.

Our connection, once bound by the game's frame,
Now roams free, uncontained.
Though miles apart, in this vast space,
We found a meeting place, our own safe base.

Now, each log-in bears your name,
But our bond transcends the game.
In a friendship that flows from screen to soul,
Beyond the game, we are made whole.

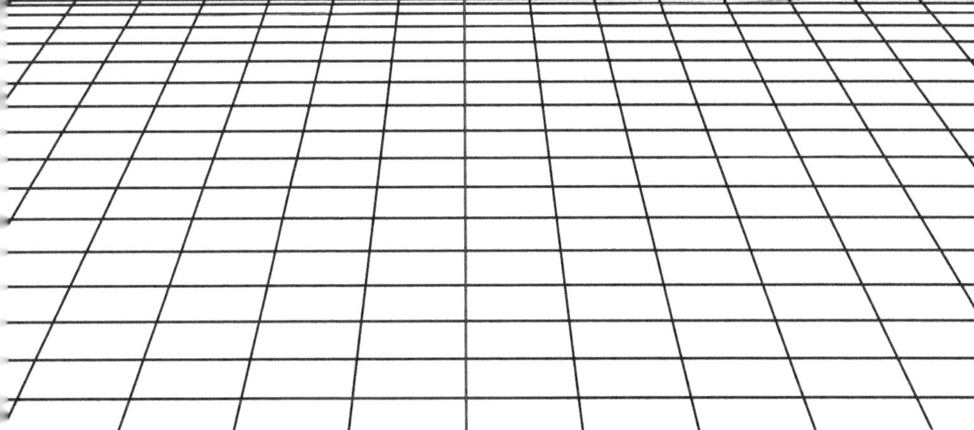

THE GOOD, THE BAD, AND THE BULLY

In a world full of avatars that roam,
Through pixelated worlds, their second home,
There lies a tale of the good and bad,
And the bullies who make the gaming sad

The Good:

Knights of honor in digital form,
Banding together through every storm.
Heroes who heal, who guard, who save,
In every quest, valiant and brave.

They share their loot, they guide the new,
Creating bonds firm, deep, and true.
In guilds and parties, they stand as one,
Celebrating victories, battles won.

The Bad:

Yet, shadows linger in these virtual lands,
Crafted by less benevolent hands.
Tricksters and trolls with mischief sown,
Seeding chaos, a tone overblown.

They hack and cheat, steal and lie,
Sowing discord, as tempers fly.
A duel of words, a test of wills,
The bad actors, with dubious skills.

The Bully:

But the darkest player in this game,
Is the bully, calling names.
They prey on fears, they taunt, they jeer,
Turning what should be fun into something to fear.

They mock and belittle, they harass and harry,
Making the atmosphere tense and wary.
Yet, in this world, they too are known,
Not as kings, but thrones overthrown.

MESSAGES AND CALLS

At first, a ping—a simple sign,
From the game to a message line.
Words in bubbles, light and brief,
Tidbits shared, in disbelief.

Our screens—once battlegrounds, now a bridge,
Connecting more than just a mid-game ridge.
Texts pinged nightly 'neath the stars,
Our words danced between avatars.

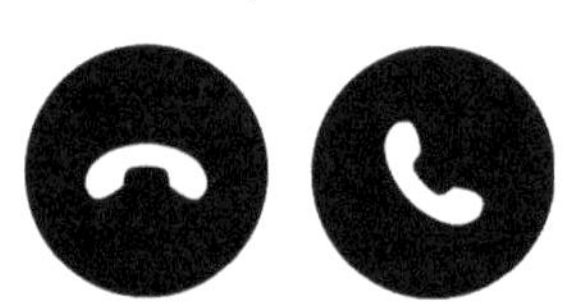

Voices ventured, shy and slight,
Across digital waves, through cyber night.
Calls lingered on as hours passed,
In talks of nothing meant to last.

Yet, in that nothing, something grew,
A cord of trust, subtly true.
From casual chats to confessions deep,
Secrets sown, for us to keep.

Echoes of laughter, soft and clear,
Through speakers whispering, peer to peer.
Each call, each message, our bridge extends,
Beyond the game, where friendship blends.

We found in digital tones a path,
Where jokes, and dreams, and sorrows hath.
A line from heart to heart was cast,
With each call, each message, vast

Pixels in Jest

A virtual world where jesters play,
A laugh, a trick, another way,
To lighten hearts with digital pranks,
In chat rooms filled with jests and thanks.

With potions mixed in playful spite,
Or sudden scares that shock and delight,
Each trick a laugh, wrapped in a riddle,
Setting off a chain, a prankster's fiddle.

Hidden traps in pixelated paths,
Unexpected turns, and virtual laughs.
A misplaced object, a sudden slide,
Moments where we can't help but abide.

Teammates turned to playful foes,
With every prank, our friendship grows.
Laughter echoes through digital halls,
Uniting us as it gently enthralls.

In every session, jest finds its place,
Brightening the pixels of cyber space.
Through pranks we bond, through games we share,
In every mischievous trick, a care.

A world so serious needs a light touch,
And in our game, pranks mean so much.
For in laughter, we find a common ground,
Where joy and camaraderie are found.

THE GREAT CYBER CHASE

In the glow of screens, we play a game,
A digital hide and seek of names and claims.
Emotions tucked behind icons and memes,
Echoing softly in the streams.

You hide a smile in a well-placed joke,
I seek the truth behind the smoke.
A laughing emoji, a witty retort,
Behind each, a feeling of a different sort.

We navigate through chats and posts,
Hiding in plain sight, almost ghosts.
Peeking through the curtains of digital plays,
Seeking signs in the virtual maze.

I dodge, you weave, through coded lines,
A dance of pixels, signs, and rhymes.
What's real or masked in this playful chase,
In every tag, a hidden face.

Yet, as we play this seeking game,
The rules blur, no longer the same.
Feelings emerge, real and stark, 
In the moments we find in the dark.

From heart to heart, the signals send,
No longer just a game to pretend.
In digital hide and seek, we find,
Not just feelings left behind, but intertwined.

Unfiltered Moments

In the spaces between staged smiles,
Lies the truth of our unfettered miles.
Unfiltered moments, raw and real,
Capture the essence of what we truly feel.

No gloss, no edits, no careful pose,
Just the natural rhythm, as life's current flows.
A laugh that bursts, unbidden, free,
A tear that falls, for only you to see.

These are the snapshots of deeper tales,
Beyond the reach of perfect veils.
The coffee spilled on morning's rush,
The silent peace in evening's hush.

A hand held in a quiet need,
A wordless glance, a shared creed.
Life, unpolished, without a frame,
Beautiful in its unvarnished claim.

In these moments, truth finds its voice,
In the chaos, the mess, the noise.
Unfiltered, untouched by any screen,
Showing us what authenticity means.

So let us cherish these unfiltered scenes,
For life is lived in the in-betweens.
Where perfection meets the imperfect test,
In unfiltered moments, life shows its best.

THE GAME CONTINUES

In a kingdom where legends rise and fall,
Our avatars persist, through every call.
Beyond mere pixels, our spirits soar,
In quests we face, and lore we explore.

Together, we traverse fantasy lands,
Our fates entwined by digital strands.
Yet as we play, a parallel tale unfolds,
One of us, not characters in roles.

With every boss defeated, every level gained,
Our friendship deepens, unrestrained.
In chats that span from dusk till dawn,
The game continues, our bond reborn.

In this shared space where we both flee,
Life's trials mimic those we see on screen.
Challenges met with combined might,
In virtual battles and real-life plights.

As seasons change in worlds both fair and foul,
Our connection proves more than avatars allow.
The game is our beginning, not our end,
Through every update, every extend.

let us play, let mysteries unfold,
In games and life, let stories be told.
The screen lights our faces with its glow,
The game continues, and so we grow

Section Three: Heartbeats in Code

DIGITAL HEARTBEATS

The virtual code that gave us light,
Our hearts synced in digital night.
Across vast networks, through wires and waves,
Our emotions surged, no longer slaves.

Conversations deep in the pixel glow,
Revealing more than avatars show.
Each text, each ping, a pulse felt deep,
Digital heartbeats, no longer asleep.

From laughter shared in typed-out lines
To comforting words in trying times,
Each message sent, a heartbeat quick,
In the quiet clicks of a mouse, a flick.

We shared dreams within our coded land,
Woven tightly by strands of broadband.
Not just data, not mere bytes,
But heartbeats encoded in our digital nights.

In every game, beneath every quest,
Our true selves test, confessed, expressed.
No longer mere players in a scripted scene,
But hearts connected, through a screen.

As we navigate this virtual space,
Our heartbeats find a common place.
In every login, every nightly meet,
Our pulses dance, in sync, complete.

Virtual Refuge

In the quiet corners of my room,
The screen flickers, a beacon in the gloom.
Amidst the chaos of the world outside,
In pixels and quests, I find a place to hide.

A realm where dragons soar and heroes rise,
Underneath these digital skies,
My avatar runs through fields of gold,
In this world, my fears are put on hold.

Each login, a gateway to escape,
From life's relentless, grinding scrape.
In battles fought with friends by side,
The real world's sadness, briefly denied.

Joy blooms in every victory won,
Underneath this electronic sun.
With each level up, my spirits lift,
In this virtual world, I find my gift.

The laughter shared with allies true,
Brings light to skies once darkened hue.
Though pixels fade as sessions end,
In this game, I find the will to mend.

A refuge from reality's sharp claws,
In coded realms, I pause my flaws.
Here, joy displaces every sorrow,
Giving strength to face tomorrow.

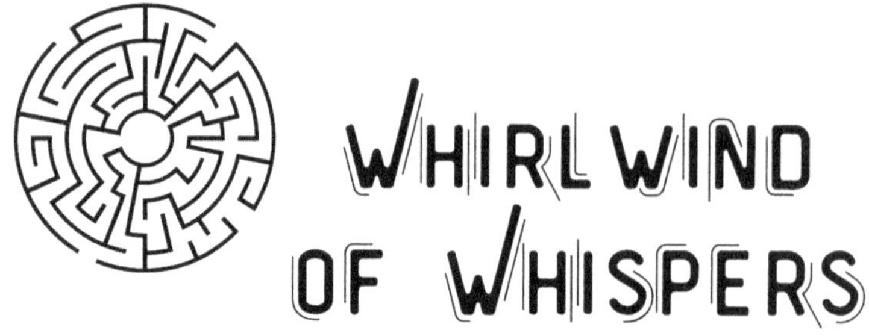

WHIRLWIND OF WHISPERS

In the maze of my mind, whispers twirl,
A tapestry of thoughts, unfurled.
Emotions tangled like threads on a loom,
In the quiet chaos of my heart's own room.

Feelings rise like tides against the shore,
Each wave clashes, then pulls once more.
Love? Fear? A blend so sweet and sour,
Each minute laced with a different power.

Your words, a melody that sways and bends,
Within each note, a message sends.
But clarity fades in the echo's dance,
Leaving my heart in a delicate trance.

What is this feeling? So sharp, so keen,
A slicing breeze, unseen, unclean.
A storm of maybe, a gust of might,
Darkness and light in endless fight.

Do you feel it too, this tangled skein?
Or am I alone with my joy and pain?
A puzzle missing half its pieces,
This riddle of emotion never ceases.

Yet still, I tread through this intricate fog,
Guided by the light of an internal monologue.
Hoping that clarity will come to pass,
In the mirror of my soul's looking glass.

Pixeled Heart to Real Heartbeats

The day dawned like any other,
My heart locked away, under cover.
Yet in the glow of my flickering screen,
A whisper of something, previously unseen.

Your words, once pixels, now a touch so real,
Against my stern resolve, they gently peel.
The cautious barriers built over time,
Eroded by your digital chime.

In the quiet hum of our shared space,
My defenses faltered, seeing your virtual face.
With each joke shared, each secret told,
The warmth seeped in, the cold grew old.

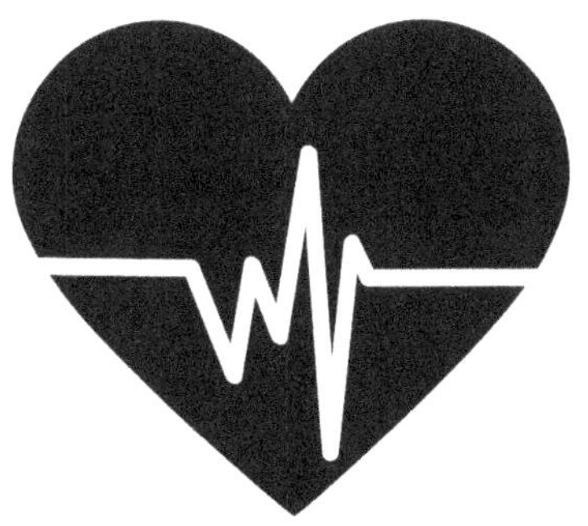

It was not in grand gestures or passionate pleas,
But in a gentle nudge, a soft, sweet tease.
That I found my heart giving way,
To the digital love I denied day by day.

So I typed the words, letting the truth flow,
Releasing feelings I'd dared not show.
"I'm yours," I wrote, a simple line,
Surrendering to the love defined by online.

From that moment, the world shifted slight,
Our digital love casting a new light.
No longer a game, or pixels on a display,
But a true connection, here to stay.

Awaiting the Digital Dawn

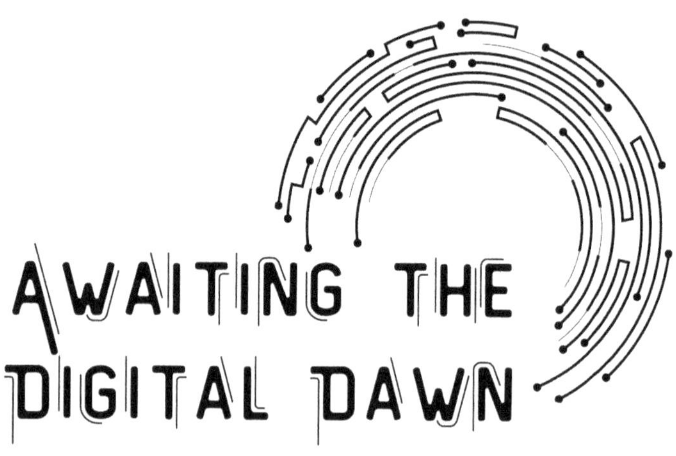

Each minute stretches, a tiny eternity,
As I watch the screen, waiting for you to be.
The cursor blinks, a steady beat,
In the silence of this empty seat.

The green light of your digital presence,
A beacon of hope, of pleasant essence.
Yet until it shines, my world's a little dim,
Hanging on the verge of a whimsical whim.

Notifications tease with every ping,
But it's you I await, for my heart to sing.
Friends chatter through pixels and code,
Yet my screen feels empty, a desolate road.

This quiet vigil, by the keyboard's glow,
Where once we danced, in a digital show.
Your words, a melody, so vivid and clear,
Now I'm just waiting, wishing you were here.

Time ticks away, each second a sigh,
Caught in the limbo, between low and high.
Will you appear with your usual flair,
To dispel the shadows, the weight of the air?

My heart leaps at each momentary flicker,
Hope surges strong, then fades quicker.
This digital doorstep, where I quietly pine,
Hoping to see the sign that you're online.

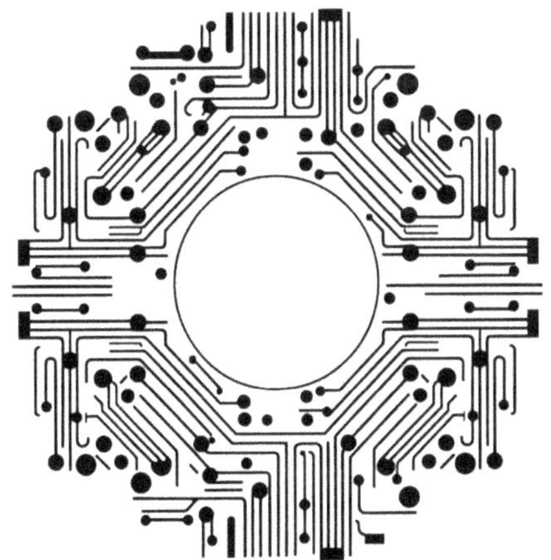

The Promise of Reality

In the glow of screens late into the night,
We speak of dreams, of taking flight
From the digital realms where we roam,
To a future where fantasies become home.

Beneath the flicker of virtual skies,
We map out where our true hopes lie.
A promise whispered through digital streams,
Binding us closer than it seems.

From texts to talks, from pixels to breath,
The promise of reality weaves beneath;
A bridge from the virtual to the tactile space,
Where we envision meeting face to face.

Our words, a pact sealed in binary,
Hold the weight of a future, barely seen.
Not just avatars but flesh and bone,
The promise of touching the unknown.

We count the days, the hours, the minutes,
Till the digital fades and reality begins it.
A meeting set where virtual ends,
And the promise of reality transcends.

SECTION FOUR: CRACKS IN THE CODE

Pixels of Joy

In the vast, virtual expanse we played,
Creating moments, bright and arrayed.
Laughter echoed through digital halls,
In games and chats, where joy recalls.

Memories crafted in online quests,
Where friendships formed at their very best.
Screens lit with smiles, eyes agleam,
Sharing joys in a flowing stream.

Each login a return to shared delight,
Where avatars danced into the night.
A treasure hunt, a battle won,
Under the watchful eye of a pixel sun.

Jokes typed in quick succession,
Finding humor in every session.
Happy accidents, serendipity's play,
In digital worlds, where we chose to stay.

Screenshots saved of victorious days,
Frozen moments in the cyber maze.
These pixels of joy, small and bright,
Keep our spirits aloft in flight.

As we log off, the warmth remains,
In the heart's cache, where happiness reigns.
For in this digital space we find,
Happy memories that forever bind.

CRACKS IN THE CODE

In the code of our connection,
Subtle errors begin their quiet inflection.
Lines once seamless, now subtly fray,
Signals cross in unexpected ways.

Where laughter flowed, a silence falls,
Echoing strangely within digital walls.
Messages delayed, replies run cold,
The warmth we shared becomes unexpectedly old.

A glitch in our system, unseen, profound,
Disrupts the harmony we thought sound.
Pixels blur where clarity reigned,
In the code of our bond, an error stained.

Jokes once shared now miss their mark,
Leaving behind a growing dark.
Smiles that lit our screens before,
Now the light flickers, joy no more.

Each login a chore, not a delight,
As our avatars drift further from sight.
The game we played feels tiresome, sad,
A stark contrast to the joy we had.

In the architecture of our virtual place,
Cracks widen in once-sturdy space.
Yet, through the fault lines, a truth makes call,
To mend or end, lest deeper we fall.

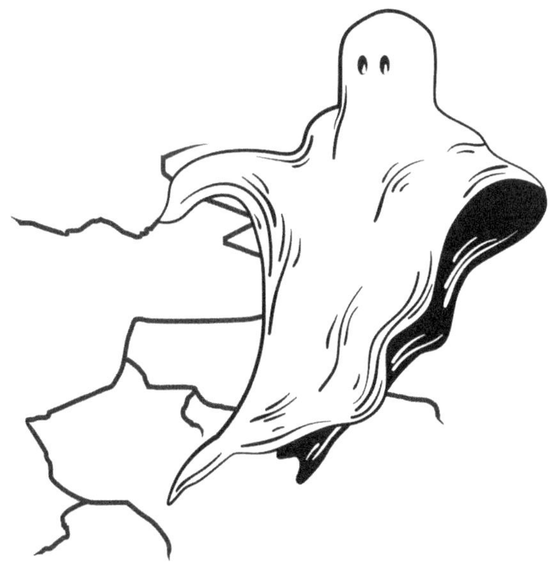

LAG AND DISCONNECTS

In the silence between sent and seen,
Lies a lag, a gap, where words once been.
Typed in haste or with careful thought,
Messages hang—received, or perhaps not.

Echoes of our digital tone,
Once so clear, now barely known.
Lag stretches, a gulf wide and deep,
In the pauses, doubts begin to creep.

Disconnects in our coded chat,
Where once was dialogue, now flat.
Frustration builds with each missed beat,
A syncing error we cannot defeat.

Our conversation once a lively stream,
Now stutters like a broken dream.
Each attempt to connect seems to fail,
With every error, our spirits pale.

Reboot, retry, messages resend,
Wishing only for this lag to end.
But the gap widens, as does the strain,
In the static, we feel the pain.

What once was easy, now a chore,
To bridge the disconnect we once ignored.
Can we debug this growing glitch,
Or is this the point where we switch?

Buffering hearts need time to load,
Yet fear the moment they might explode.
In the space between our digital words,
Lies the sorrow of unheard chords.

MISUNDERSTOOD MESSAGES

Words typed in haste, a screen aglow,
Intended meanings lost in digital flow.
Messages sent across the void,
Once clarity, now paranoid.

Emoticons meant to soften a word,
Interpreted as something absurd.
A joke falls flat, its humor unseen,
Replaced by a question, "What do you mean?"

In the virtual haze, our words collide,
Intentions good, but impact wide.
Phrases once benign, now seeds of doubt,
Misunderstandings sprout about.

Each notification, a pulse of dread,
"What if it's something else," we said.
The simplest texts spiral out of control,
Misread sentiments taking their toll.

Can we decode this tangled script,
Find where our connection slipped?
Or are we destined to misconstrue,
What's meant to bind, not to undo?

Parsing through each sentence, each line,
Seeking a sign in the lexical brine.
Hoping to clarify, rectify the breach,
With a message clear, one within reach

In this realm where words are all,
Misunderstood messages, our downfall.
Yet still, we type, we send, we yearn,
For the day when our words return.

The Unwanted Merge

In the realm where virtual warriors stride,
Where kingdoms stand side by side,
An echo of change disrupts the peace—
A server merge, a forced release.

Once separate worlds, now forcefully twined,
Unwanted merge, players resigned.
Familiar faces, now thronged by strangers,
In the digital realm, facing new dangers.

Guilds once mighty, now scramble to blend,
Old rivalries clash, alliances bend.
Territories expand, borders dissolve,
As new overlords attempt to solve.

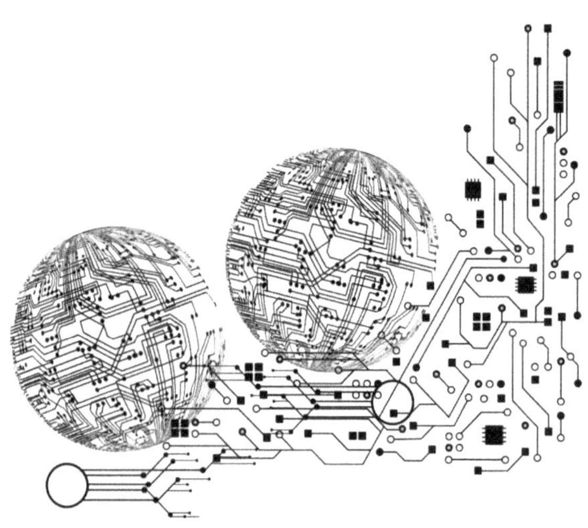

Chat rooms buzz with unrest and dismay,
Veteran players lament the day.
Strategies upturned, landscapes reformed,
A community's fabric, oddly transformed.

In this forced union, some find strength,
New friendships forge at extended length.
Yet others yearn for the days of old,
When stories were theirs to tell, bold and uncontrolled.

A digital world, forever changed,
Players adapt, strategies rearranged.
The unwanted merge, a new chapter begins,
In the game of pixels, who loses, who wins?

SERVER DOWN

The screen freezes, cursor blinking in place,
A sudden halt in our digital embrace.
"Server down," the cold message reads,
A stark echo of our unmet needs.

Lost connection, a spinning wheel,
Reflects how disconnected we feel.
Attempts to reconnect, to revive the spark,
In growing shadows, ever stark.

Frantic clicks, a desperate plea,
Wishing it were simple, for you and me.
To reboot, restore, what once was clear,
Before the silence, before the fear.

Lines of communication abruptly cut,
Leaves us stranded in a mutual rut.
No error message for the heart,
Just a blank screen, torn apart.

Memories buffer in the mind's eye,
Of better days, now passed by.
When laughter flowed through wires and
air,
Now static fills the despair.

Is there a patch, a fix, a code,
To reset the path, to lighten the load?
Or do we accept the dreaded truth,
Our connection lost, its vitality couth?

In the quiet aftermath of the crash,
Amid the flicker of hope and ash,
We wait for signals, for a sign,
That our server will come back online.

SECTION FIVE: THE PARTING

Am I a pawn in your digital game,
Or just a player in the same?
Each message sent, each call you make,
Feels like a move that's hard to take.

Are we spinning in a cycle of play,
Where emotions twist and sway?
Your words come like a summer rain,
Sweet and fresh, but with hidden pain.

I parse each text, each emoji's face,
Searching for a clue, a trace.
Is there truth behind your digital smile,
Or am I just lost in a tech-savvy guile?

Your presence is a ghost on my screen,
Nowhere solid, yet somehow seen.
Are you real, or just a facade,
A beautiful illusion, a heartfelt nod?

I'm caught in a web of pixels and texts,
Trying to decipher what comes next.
Am I being played? Or do I willingly stay,
In a game where emotions are the ultimate play?

This game we play, so intricate and deep,
Leaves my heart in a leap.
Am I being played? Do I even care?
Or is the thrill of the game too sweet to bear?

A WAITING GAME

In the quiet glow of my waiting screen,
I sit, hoping for a sign to be seen.
A ghost in the machine, you promised to play,
But hours tick by, fading into gray.

The digital world, once a playground wide,
Now echoes empty where shadows reside.
I type, I wait, my heart on display,
For the ghost who promised, but stayed away.

Messages drafted, then erased,
A conversation paused, lost in cyberspace.
Each login a hope, each logout a sigh,
A cycle of waiting, under the digital sky.

The games we played, the laughs we shared,
Now distant memories, as if you never cared.
I'm left questioning what was real,
In a game where emotions are hard to feel.

The avatar of you, once bright and near,
Now just a ghost, disappearing clear.
Did you forget, or just decide,
That the game was over, no need to hide?

I'm waiting still, for a ghost to appear,
To press 'play' on emotions left in arrear.
But the screen stays dark, the game undone,
The ghost has vanished, the waiting won.

THE LAST LOG-IN

The screen lights up one final time,
A portal to memories, bittersweet and prime.
Your avatar stands there, silent and still,
A digital echo of a vanishing will.

The last log-in, a quiet goodbye,
No fanfare, just a sigh.
A cursor blinks in the hollow room,
Counting down moments to impending gloom.

Messages sent, now drift in the void,
Echoes of a bond, once enjoyed.
Each keystroke a heavy, laden feel,
Typing out emotions we can no longer conceal.

How did we come to this somber end,
Where once a message was enough to send
Waves of joy across the bytes and bits,
Now just digital remnants, the puzzle fits.

Your status darkens, "last seen" fades,
As into the network, your presence wades.
A logout click, so soft, so slight,
The end of our story, into the night.

But in this last log-in, there's an unspoken plea,
A hope that maybe, you'll remember me.
As more than pixels, more than data streams,
In the quiet corners of your digital dreams.

SILENCE AFTER SIGN-OFF

The final message sent, then silence falls,
A deafening stillness within digital walls.
The glowing screen, once alive with your words,
Now darkens to quiet, undisturbed.

The buzzing notifications cease,
In their absence, a strange peace.
But beneath the calm, a storm does brew,
A hollow feeling, born of missing you.

The chat window, a vacant frame,
Echoes with the remnants of your name.
Each icon, each emoji we used to send,
Marks the map of a journey's end.

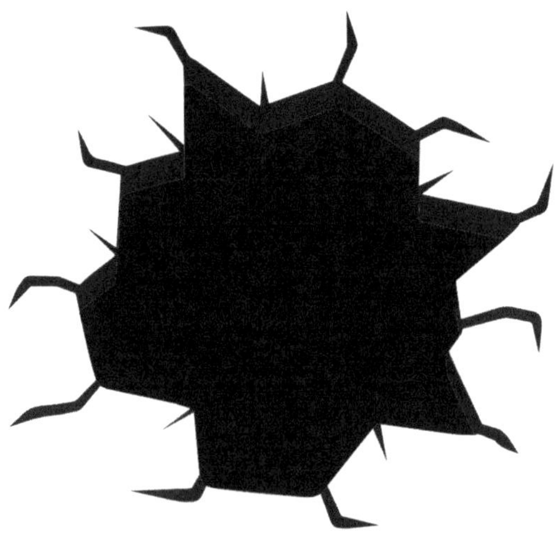

Silence stretches, taut and thin,
A void where laughter once had been.
The room feels colder, slightly off,
As memories echo with each soft cough.

A sign-off, a simple click,
Can sever connections, quick and slick.
But the silence left behind is vast,
Filled with shadows of the past.

I sit and watch the cursor blink,
In the silence, I'm left to think.
Of all the words we shared before,
Now just echoes on the digital shore.

Silence after sign-off, a poignant close,
A chapter ends, a story goes.
Yet in the quiet, I hold dear,
The hope that your words might
reappear.

Unsent Messages

In the draft folder lie words unspoken,
Unsent messages, tokens of emotion
broken.
Each line a whisper of what could have
been,
Each pause a story, unseen, serene.

Hovering over 'send,' a moment's
hesitation,
A heart's debate, a quiet contemplation.
Fear intertwines with the desire to share,
Tangled thoughts, floating in digital air.

Memories drafted in hurried script,
Deleted, revised, then cautiously clipped.
Words that burn with truth's fierce flame,
Too potent to send, too real to name.

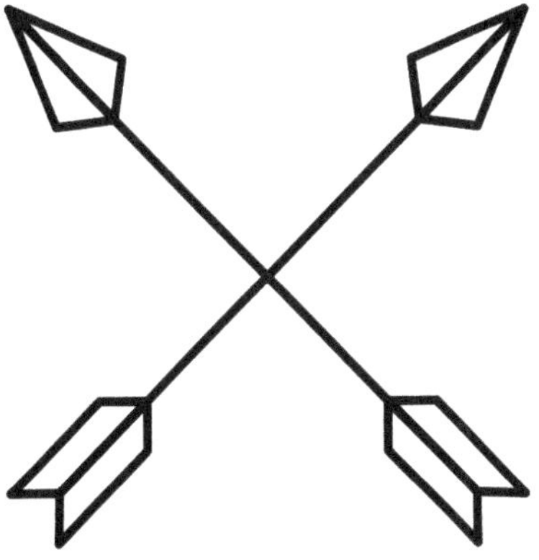

The 'send' button glows, an invitation,
To bridge the gap, a communication.
Yet they remain, these silent missives,
Invisible weight, persistent, passive.

How many emotions left to linger here,
In the cold mechanics of this digital sphere?
Love, regret, anger, confession,
All paused at the edge of expression.

Unsent messages, a collection vast,
Each one a ghost from the recent past.
Hovering in the space between,
Forever written, never seen.

SECTION SIX: ECHOES

GHOST IN THE MACHINE

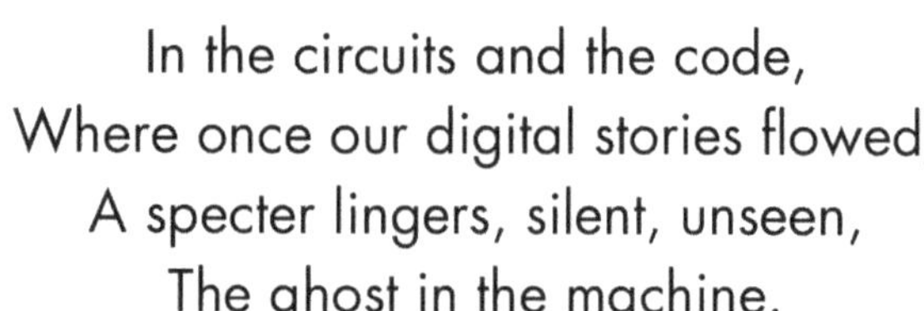

In the circuits and the code,
Where once our digital stories flowed,
A specter lingers, silent, unseen,
The ghost in the machine.

Once vibrant with your avatars,
Now empty spaces, like distant stars.
Your laughter echoes, a fading sound,
In chat rooms where we once were found.

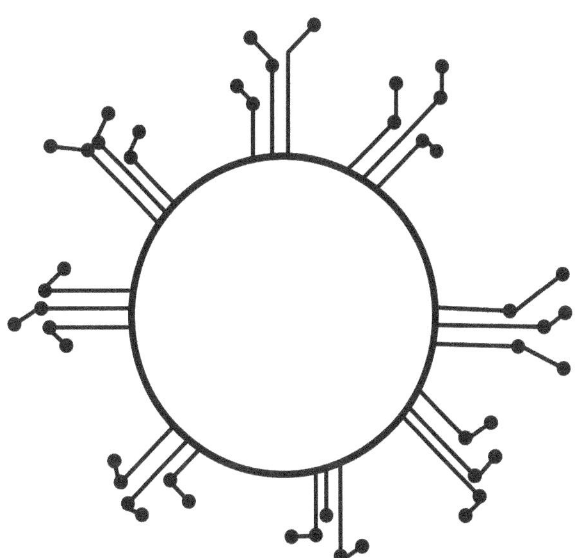

Each login feels a little cold,
Navigating files, folders old.
Your data, like a digital shroud,
Drifts like mist, a lingering cloud.

Notifications have ceased to chime,
Yet your presence transcends time.
In every pixel, every line,
The ghost of you, forever mine.

Memories replay, a glitch in the stream,
Pixels stutter where you once gleam.
A phantom touch in the data's embrace,
A hollow where I still see your face.

I search for you in our shared space,
Finding traces of your digital trace.
A file, a photo, left behind,
Footprints of a virtual kind.

Ghost in the machine, you haunt my screen,
In the quiet bytes, your essence seen.
Though you've logged off, moved beyond,
In the machine, your ghost lives on.

To Fight or Not for Love

The war in my heart of our affection,
Where whispers clash and hearts seek direction,
The question lingers, heavy and profound:
Should I fight for love, or let go, unbound?

Each moment together, stitched with golden thread,
Yet shadows loom, weaving doubt instead.
Love, once bright, now a flickering flame,
Should I stoke the fire, or abandon the game?

To fight for love—is to challenge the storm,
To embrace the winds, and transform.
A test of strength, of courage, of heart,
A pact to try, a vow not to part.

Yet, when is the struggle too steep to endure?
When do the scars not hint at a cure?
Not all battles promise a prize worth the pain,
Not all storms cease, not all endings gain.

This tormenting balance of loss and gain,
A heart's gamble, love's own domain.
Do we hold fast, do we stake our claim,
Or release our grip, leaving love to wane?

So here we stand, you and I, at love's precipice,
Pondering if the fight is worth the bliss.
Is it braver to hold on, or let go,
To free our bonds and thus, truly know?

Shadows in the Chatroom

In the dim light of a forgotten chatroom,
Echoes stir, a whisper, a phantom loom.
Once alive with words, a fervent flow,
Now silent as the forgotten snow.

Shadows linger where we used to speak,
In the corners where the pixels leak.
Your laughter, once a vivid hue,
Now just a shadow, a residue.

Each message sent, a fading trace,
A memory locked in digital space.
The room holds tight to every byte,
Shadows of our shared delight.

The cursor blinks in a rhythmic beat,
A heartbeat in the abandoned suite.
I type a word, then erase the start,
A futile attempt to bridge what's apart.

The chatroom, a relic of a time once dear,
Holds the shadows of those no longer here.
A virtual cave of echoes, dim and vast,
Where shadows whisper of the past.

I linger, lost, in the spectral light,
Amidst the ghosts of conversations, quiet.
The chatroom holds its breath, then sighs,
A place where digital warmth never dies.

SILENT SIGNALS

Silent screen, a static glow,
Once a fountain, now forlorn.
Each message sent, like a stone in a well,
Echoes down, with no tale to tell.

The chime of hope, now seldom heard,
A waiting game, undisturbed.
Texts dispatched to the void unseen,
A digital limbo, cold and lean.

What weight carries an unread note?
A sinking ship, or a castaway's boat?
Floating in the ether, adrift and spare,
Words like ghosts, suspended in air.

Ignored messages, a quiet plea,
Read me, see me, remember me.
Yet the silence looms, vast and wide,
A gulf between, with nowhere to hide.

Each ignored call, a brick in the wall,
A barrier rises, tall and appall.
Once open gates, now firmly closed,
Paths diverge, futures opposed.

In this realm where words are king,
Ignored messages, a silent sting.
A digital pain, sharp and precise,
A cold reminder of a rolling dice.

Do they pierce the heart, these unseen reads?
Or fade away, like unwatered seeds?
Only time will tell, in the echo's wake,
The cost of silence, the heartache it makes.

ECHOES OF EMOTICONS

In the quiet aftermath of our digital words,
Linger the echoes of emoticons, heard
In the spaces between what we used to say,
Smiles and frowns left to decay.

A smiley face, a tear, a wink,
Carried more than one might think.
Each symbol, a capsule of mood and tone,
Now silent echoes in the zone.

They danced across the screen in play,
Brightening texts day by day.
But now they float like ghosts, bereft,
Remnants of the emotions left.

A laughing face, echoes of glee,
A sorrowful tear, once shared with me.
In each, a memory, vividly drawn,
Of conversations, now long gone.

How strange these digital traces seem,
Faint reminders of a dream.
In the gallery of chat, they stand,
Echoes of a distant land.

Each emoticon, a stroke of heart,
A small art piece, a tiny part
Of the tapestry we wove online,
Now but echoes left behind.

THE FRAGILITY OF PROMISES

We stitched promises on the edges of night,
Under stars that witnessed our plight.
Words woven with the threads of our dreams,
Floating on breezes, silent screams.

Promises painted like dawn's first light,
Promising forever, holding tight.
Yet as the sun climbs, so too the truth,
That some oaths are frail, not bulletproof.

These pledges, like leaves in the wind,
Dance with a grace that's paper-thin.
They fly, they flutter, beautifully weak,
Spoken with a fire, extinguished as we speak.

We make them with the best of intent,
But intentions bend, and wills are spent.
Promises that, like glass, might shatter,
Showing us that truth is what truly matters.

So when they break, these fragile vows,
Do not think of the whys or hows.
For some promises are delicate art,
Meant to be broken, right from the start.

A lesson in each fragmented piece,
That from broken things, we find release.
For not all bonds are meant to stay,
Some are just whispers, carried away

SECTION SEVEN: THE PRESENCE OF ABSENCE

OFFLINE STATUS

Your name, once a beacon, now dims,
A simple status, offline, at the whim
Of life's unpredictable, swift course,
A sudden silence, a dissonant force.

Where once your icon glowed with life,
Now stillness reigns, cutting like a knife.
A small gray dot, a quiet end,
No more messages to send.

Each time I log in, hope sparks, then fades,
As your offline shadow in the margins wades.
A digital ghost in the machine,
A memory, felt but not seen.

Your absence looms, large and stark,
In chat rooms now silent, once vibrant parks.
I hover over the option to ping,
But retreat, knowing no reply it will bring.

How heavy this offline weight,
A reminder of a sealed fate.
No logins, no updates, no trace,
Just empty space in your usual place.

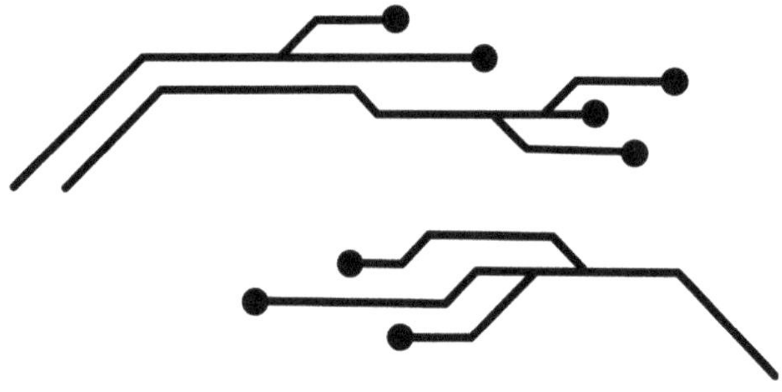

Yet in this digital quiet, I sense,
Echoes of laughter, your presence intense.
For though offline your status remains,
In my heart, your spirit sustains.

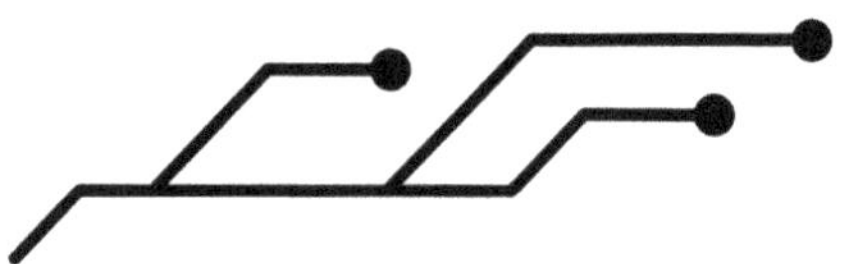

THE SPACE BETWEEN PIXELS

In the quiet lulls of our online realm,
Where words are typed but not overwhelmed,
Lies the space between pixels, fine and thin,
Holding the essence of what might have been.

This gap, not seen but deeply felt,
Where emotions simmer, hearts melt.
A pixelated barrier, yet within, a bridge,
Spanning our worlds, mile to ridge.

Through these screens, we reach, we touch,
In the space between, we share so much.
More than data, more than bytes,
In these gaps, our spirit alights.

Messages travel across this void,
In digital whispers, hopes employed.
Yet it's in these silences, these pauses long,
That our unseen bonds grow strong.

The space between pixels, a canvas vast,
For future dreams, for memories past.
A place where silent understandings lie,
Underneath the digital sky.

Though separated by screens and miles,
Connected we remain, across the aisles.
For in the space between pixelated scenes,
Lives the depth of our digital dreams.

SOLO PLAYTHROUGH

I booted up the game, a familiar screen,
But the side beside me remained unseen.
The chair empty, the headset still,
In the game we loved, I climbed the hill.

I played alone, without your cheer,
No partner in quests, just silence here.
The monsters loomed, larger without your aid,
Each victory muted, each shadow swayed.

Where once we laughed and strategized,
Only echoes of your voice, now minimized.
I moved through maps we once explored,
Alone, the joy felt underscored.

The levels passed, achievements won,
But the thrill seemed less, the fun undone.
A game shared, now a solo quest,
Missing the companion who played it best.

I played alone, and though I progressed,
The game felt different, the experience less.
For each session ends, and I realize anew,
It's not just the game, I miss playing with you.

LOSING ALL MY GAME HEARTS

In the pixelated depths of my favorite place,
I watch as my last heart disappears without a trace.
Each loss a tiny echo in a virtual expanse,
Mirroring the beats of missed chances and
circumstance.

Level by level, the challenges grew,
My confidence shaken, my options few.
The enemies stronger, the mazes more complex,
Every failure a text, subtext perplex.

I stood at the threshold of the final stage,
Armed with nothing but remnants of rage.
But one by one, my hearts slipped away,
Like stars fading at the break of day.

In the silence of a screen gone dark,
I sat, reflecting on my lost spark.
The game was over, my journey done,
No fanfare, no applause, no battles won.

Yet in the quiet of that digital defeat,
A lesson lay in the absence of a heartbeat.
Not every loss is meant to break,
Sometimes, it's just a pause, a chance to retake.

So I'll gather more hearts, restart the game,
New strategies learned, never the same.
For in every ending, there's a new start,
And losing all my game hearts is just a part.

FINAL LOGOUT

I logged out last night, turned off the screen,
Walked away from the world where I had been queen.
The realms where I ruled, the battles I fought,
All left behind, a final thought.

No more daily quests, no guild wars to wage,
I closed the chapter, turned the page.
The friends I made, the foes I faced,
In digital echoes, now erased.

The thrill of the chase, the glory of the win,
Replaced by silence, from within.
I left the game for good, a quiet retreat,
A decision firm, a feat complete.

Memories linger, bittersweet and stark,
Of flashing screens in rooms grown dark.
Yet in my heart, a newfound space,
For peace, for life, at a gentler pace.

I left the game, but not without a cost,
For something gained, something lost.
A chapter closed, a new one begins,
Life beyond the game, free of digital sin

DREAMS OF DIGITAL WORLDS

In the twilight of my screen's soft glow,
I escape to worlds that no one knows.
Digital realms where I can fly,
Beyond the earth, beneath the sky.

In this universe of zeros and ones,
Where time stops and space runs,
I build castles in the digital sand,
Crafting realities with a wave of my hand.

Fantasies spun on silicon threads,
Landscapes sprawling from my head,
Mountains rise with a click, and seas,
Are drawn as easily as a gentle breeze.

Avatars dance in pixelated grace,
In worlds unbound by time or place.
Here, dreams are more than mere illusions,
In digital worlds, they find conclusions.

I forge adventures as I roam,
In these circuits, I find my home.
Chasing quests through virtual plains,
Finding solace in digital rains.

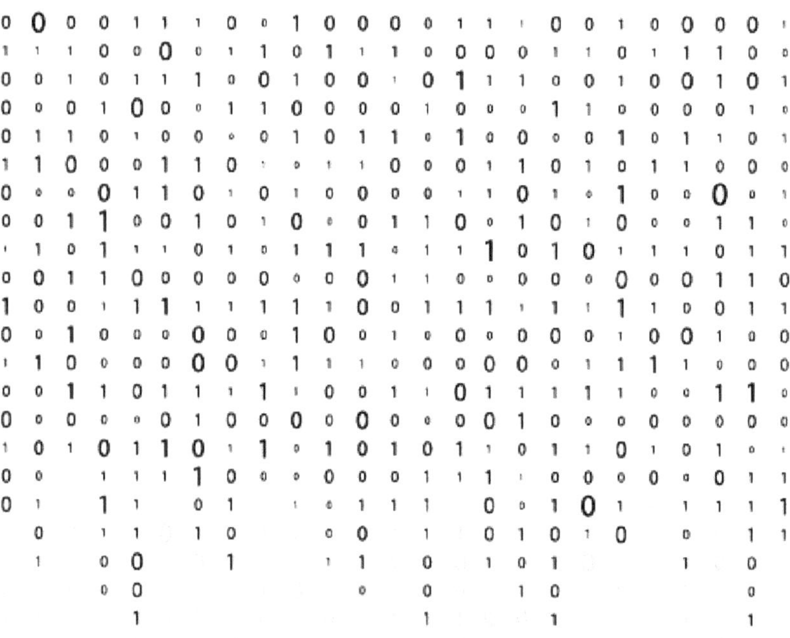

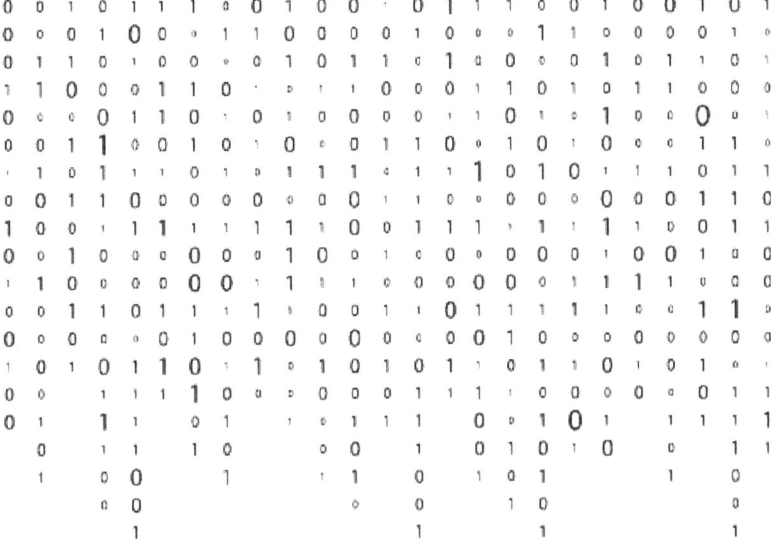

But as dawn breaks, the real calls me back,
From the depths of data, the binary black.
Yet, even as I leave my screen's embrace,
Echoes of those worlds subtly trace.

For in my mind, they continue to live,
Offering more than reality can give.
In dreams of digital worlds, I am free,
Boundless, in the vast digital sea.

SECTION EIGHT: SEASONS OF REMEMBRANCE

Spring Updates

Across the screens, a soft renewal stirs,
As winter's grip weakens and blurs.
In the digital garden, updates bloom,
Scattering the last of virtual gloom.

Icons refresh with vibrant hues,
Injecting life with springtime cues.
Operating systems shed their frost,
Old bugs fixed, files defragmented and tossed.

New features blossom, sleek and fine,
Like daffodils along the online vine.
Security patches, like rain, fall steady,
Preparing for growth, keeping us ready.

Update sync with the season,
Finding joy and fresh reasons.
Clearing clutter that winter brought,
Embracing changes, both sought and unsought.

In our chats, a lighter tone takes wing,
As we type and laugh about the coming spring.
Shared screens show landscapes bright and clear,
As we venture forth, devoid of last year's fear.

Spring updates in our digital sphere,
Mirror the renewal we hold dear.
With each reboot, restart, and refresh,
We find our spirits intertwined, enmesh.

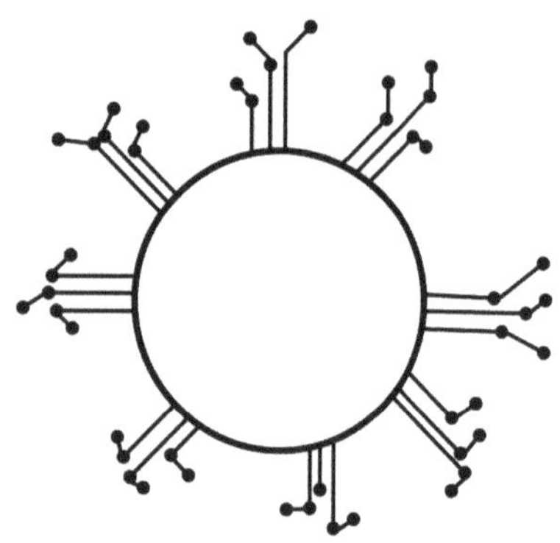

SUMMER GLITCHES

As summer heats the digital planes,
Glitches surface, data wanes.
The screens flicker with the rising sun,
Echoing the chaos, the undone.

Pixels sweat under the glaring light,
Systems strain from morning to night.
Connections falter, then revive,
A constant battle to survive.

Unexpected errors, a sudden crash,
Moments of panic, a hasty dash.
Summer's warmth brings trials anew,
In digital realms in me and you.

Yet, these glitches, though they frustrate,
Teach patience, resilience, resetting the slate.
For even in breakdowns, there's a chance to learn,
To troubleshoot, grow, and to discern.

Through each overheat, each stubborn fault,
I find the strength in our digital vault.
And as the summer storms roll in,
We brace, reboot, and begin again.

Despite the glitches, I find a way,
To laugh, to share, to continue the play.
For summer's fire, though it tests our means,
Also brings life, growth, vibrant scenes.

I navigate these glitches, side by side,
With perseverance as our guide.
Embracing summer, with all its sparks,
Finding beauty, even in its marks.

AUTUMN'S LOG-OUT

As leaves turn gold, then ember-red,
A quiet whisper through the thread,
Autumn's breath, a softer logout,
From summer's loud, vibrant shout.

Screens dim as days grow short,
Sunlight fades, a quiet retort.
Logs of green now logs of fire,
Burning bright, a natural pyre.

With each leaf that hits the ground,
A memory drops, soft without sound.
The air crisps, a cool login,
To a season of change, from without, within.

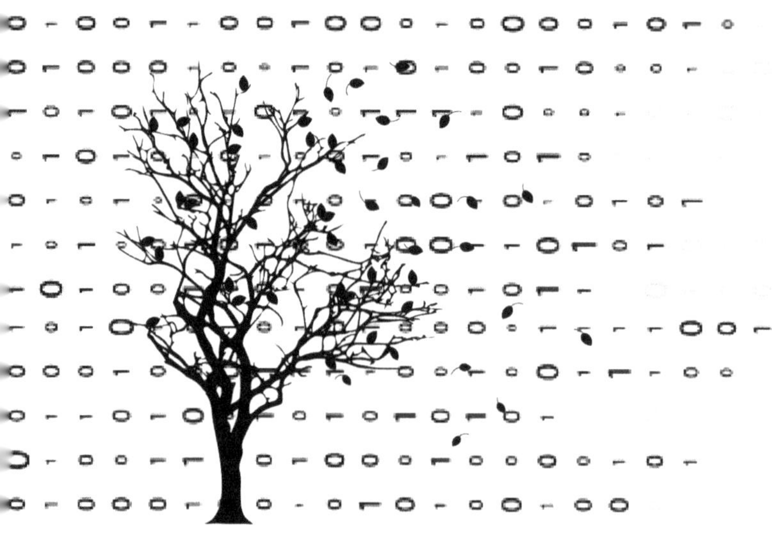

Files of mind need sorting through,
Old tasks end, new tasks queue.
Autumn teaches the art of letting go,
Of past leaves, past glories, in its slow mellow.

Yet, in this logout, there is no end,
Only pause, mend, and the chance to tend.
A logout not from presence, but from pace,
A needed shift, a new interface.

As we sync with autumn's quiet cool,
I find peace in this seasonal lull.
Logged out from summer's demanding glare,
I reboot, refreshed, repaired.

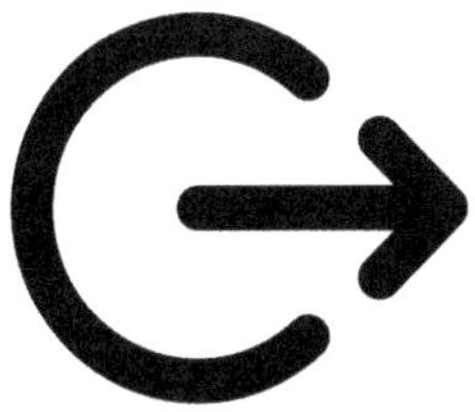

WINTER'S QUIET SERVERS

In the depth of winter's embrace,
The world slows, a quieter place.
Servers hum with a muted glow,
Preserving heat as cold winds blow.

The digital landscape, frosted and still,
Activity paused on this icy hill.
Data streams slow, a gentle crawl,
As winter's blanket covers all.

Files hibernate in cloud-stored dreams,
Waiting in silence, in frozen streams.
Updates pending, but now on hold,
As the servers rest, in the cold.

A time for maintenance, a scan, a check,
To clear the cache, a seasonal tech.
Ensuring efficiency for the year ahead,
While the world outside tucks into bed.

The quiet is profound, deep and clear,
A space for reflection on the past year.
Winter's servers, in their silent run,
Offer peace rarely found under the sun.

This stillness, a gift not often sought,
In life's fast lanes, constantly wrought.
But here in the cold, in the quiet dim,
We find strength in the digital hymn.

So let the servers softly hum,
In winter's quiet, their work not done.
Preserving, preparing, in the frosty night,
For the return of data, of light.

THE GAME I USED TO PLAY

Back when the days were long and light,
I found solace in pixels, in fights and flight.
In a world confined by the edge of a screen,
I battled, I built, I became a queen.

The game I used to play, oh, it knew me well,
From the triumph in victory to the defeat's swell.
The characters, the quests, the hidden keys,
The forests, the dungeons, the endless seas.

Hours dissolved into the ether, without a trace,
Each session a journey, a fierce embrace.
The friends who joined me on every quest,
Our laughter and tactics equally expressed

But seasons turn as they invariably do,
And the game I loved met its adieu.
New titles came, life rearranged,
Interests shifted, priorities changed.

Now, it rests in the back of my digital drawer,
A memory, a ghost of the gamer I wore.
Yet sometimes at night, when the world's asleep,
I revisit the lands where my avatar would leap.

Nostalgia grips with a bittersweet tone,
For the game I used to play, in a time long
gone.
Yet within its code, magic remains,
A part of my youth forever sustains.

Section Nine:
Healing and Hope

PATCHING THE HEART

In the workshop of my soul, quiet and dim,
I apply patches to the heart's worn rim.
Each update is a stitch, a mend, a care,
Repairing fissures from wear and tear.

Fragile threads of hope intertwined,
With the resilience of a determined mind.
The heart, like software, sometimes breaks,
Needing updates to fix its aches.

Patch by patch, we rebuild the core,
Restoring what was torn before.
Code of compassion, scripts of grace,
Written in every healed embrace.

It's not a swift process, but one of time,
Rebooting feelings, resetting the chime.
Each patch is a lesson, a memory saved,
From love, from loss, from dreams we braved.

Incremental improvements, version by new,
Each day I compile a more resilient hue.
Debugging grief, enhancing strength,
Expanding the heart's breadth and length.

Though scars may remain, they too are dear,
Markers of growth, not just of fear.
With each careful patch, the heart grows whole,
Restored in function, renewed in soul.

LESSONS FROM THE LOG FILES

In the quiet corners of the mind's drive,
Where log files store the days of my lives,
Each entry is a snippet, a moment caught,
A lesson learned, a battle fought.

Sifting through data, old and new,
Parsing errors and truths I once knew.
Each line of code, a story told,
Encoded emotions, bold or cold.

What crashes caused my systems to fail?
Which malware penetrated the protective veil?
Here in the logs, the answers wait,
Patiently revealing the turns of fate.

Analyzing moments of system stress,
Understanding more, guessing less.
Learning from the bugs of yesteryear,
To enhance the now, to clear the fear.

The log files hold not just mistakes,
But victories, joys, the high stakes.
From each, a lesson to be drawn,
Like the light that arrives with dawn.

Updating systems with newfound knowledge,
Gleaned from life's vast, intricate college.
Applying patches of wisdom and skill,
Improving the script by force of will.

Reviewing these logs once more,
Finding insights in the data store.
For each line written in my past,
Shapes the software meant to last.

REBOOTING

Press the button, hear the sound,
The system stirs from the profound.
A quiet hum, a flickering light,
Emerging from the unplanned night.

Dark screens blink into soft blue,
Clearing the old, booting the new.
A fresh start, slate wiped clean,
From the cluttered files once seen.

Rebooting after a glitch, a freeze,
A chance to rectify with ease.
Washing away the error's trace,
Setting a new, brisker pace.

In this life, I need this chance,
To reset, a renew, enhance.
From lessons learned and memories kept,
From nights I lay awake and wept.

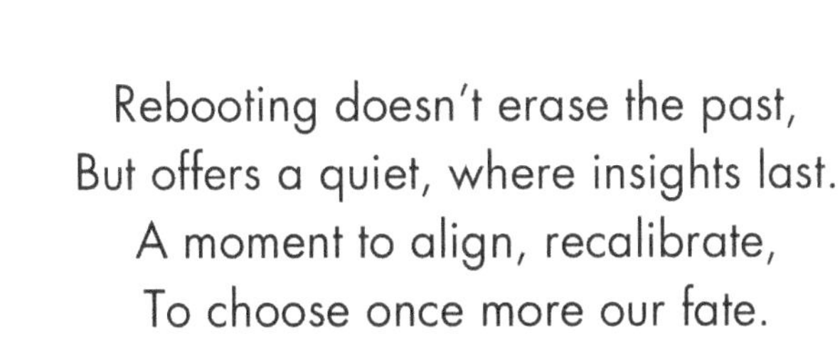

Rebooting doesn't erase the past,
But offers a quiet, where insights last.
A moment to align, recalibrate,
To choose once more our fate.

So with every sunrise, consider it so,
A reboot for the soul, letting go.
To start afresh, with new light seen,
In the warm glow of the computer screen.

NEW QUESTS AWAIT

The old world fades, a chapter closed,
My avatar rests, the servers decomposed.
A new game loads, pixels alight,
A fresh landscape unfolds in sight.

Curiosity stirs, a new adventure calls,
Unknown maps sprawl across new halls.
Characters to meet, quests to claim,
Each click a step in a different game.

The thrill of discovery in a world pristine,
Where every corner holds a scene unseen.
Skills to master, levels to beat,
A heart races with every new feat.

Yet shadows of the old game linger still,
Echoes of triumphs, the climb, the thrill.
Can this new realm ever truly feel the same?
Or is it just another board in the grander game?

But with each challenge, each victory new,
A realization grows, strong and true.
It's not the game, but how you play,
That crafts the joy, day by day.

So here I stand, at the start once more,
In a new game with worlds to explore.
A different journey, under a different name,
Life, after all, is playing another gam

CLOSING MATTER

GAME OVER

The screen fades to black, the final score displayed,
A quiet room, the echoes of battles played.
"Game Over," it reads, in stark white type,
An end to the quest, the myths, the hype.

The controller lies still in my weary hand,
Beside remnants of snacks, a solitary soda can.
The journey was long, filled with trials and tests,
Now it ends, as my avatar rests.

Memories flicker like the pixels once bright,
Adventures through digital day and digital night.
Allies and enemies, the worlds I roamed,
In this game, I found, and lost, and homed.

Each level conquered, each boss defeated,
Every achievement, bittersweet, completed.
The thrill of victory, the sting of defeat,
The music that played, ever so sweet.

Now, "Game Over," the screen solemnly declares,
But in my heart, a part of it lingers, it cares.
For every end is a start, a new game to play,
New worlds to explore, new roles to assay.

So while this chapter closes, tucked away in the
past,
The experiences, the lessons, they forever last.
A game over, yes, but not the end,
Just a pause before the next ascend.

AFTERWORD

As I close the final page of "The Ghost in the Machine: An Untold Verse Code," I'm blown away by how deep this book is. At first, I thought it was all about digital connections, but it ended up being about how technology is inextricably linked to our lives in so many ways. It's been a real journey.

I've been writing this book and it's been quite a journey of learning and thinking. The digital world is often considered a place of cold logic and data, but it's actually full of real human emotions and intricacies. Each poem in this book tries to uncover some aspect of the digital-human connection, examining how our virtual interactions affect and reflect our emotional experiences.

This book is also a testament to the power of poetry in the modern age. It challenges the notion that poetry is a dying art form, proving instead that it continues to thrive, capable of capturing the zeitgeist of our increasingly digital existence. The poems here speak to the timeless human condition through the contemporary lens of our digital lives, echoing the sentiments of those who navigate these spaces daily.

Thank you for accompanying me on this exploration of the unseen and the deeply felt, the digital and the divine. Here's to finding the poetry in our everyday clicks and keystrokes, and to recognizing the ghost in our machines—alive with verse.

About the Author

Megami Rhymes writes under the veil of anonymity, embracing the freedom to explore the depths of digital and emotional landscapes without the constraints of personal fame. While Megami may not claim the title of a polished writer, they are a fountain of fun and creative ideas, weaving stories and poems that resonate with those who venture into their imaginative realms.

Working alone, Megami has cultivated a unique voice that thrives in the solitude of creation. Their literary journey began with unpublished stories, closely guarded yet occasionally discovered by a curious sister eager to share in the creative escapades. "The Ghost in the Machine: An Untold Verse Code" is Megami's first published poetry collection, marking a bold step into the public eye with a medley of reflections on how our digital lives intertwine with genuine human emotions.

Beyond writing, Megami is an avid DIY crafter, bringing the same creativity to tangible creations as to their digital verses. Whether crafting unique home decor or handmade gifts, each project reflects Megami's passion for creating something beautiful and meaningful from scratch. This love for DIY crafts parallels the thematic crafting of their poems, each pieced together with care and ingenuity.

A devoted online gamer and a lover of crafting short love stories and poems, Megami's work invites readers to pause and ponder the powerful, often unseen connections that digital interactions can forge. This collection is not just an exploration of technology's impact on our lives but a celebration of the joy and creativity that flourish in expressing the human condition through words and crafts.

For further insights into the world of Megami Rhymes and to explore more of their creative endeavors, please visit www.selfcraftedlife.com

INVITATION FOR FEEDBACK

Your thoughts and reflections are invaluable to me. If "The Ghost in the Machine: An Untold Verse Code" has resonated with you, sparked an idea, or if you simply wish to share your own experiences with digital connections, I warmly invite you to reach out.

Please feel free to send your feedback, questions, or stories to my email at quenzcraft@gmail.com. I am eager to hear how the poems interacted with your own digital journey and to engage in meaningful discussions that may further enrich our understanding of the digital human condition.

Additionally, I encourage you to visit my website selfcraftedlife.com where you can find more information about my work, upcoming projects, and a blog where I continue exploring themes of technology, creativity, and the intersections of our digital and emotional lives. Join the conversation and become part of a community that cherishes deep, thoughtful connections.

I look forward to hearing from you and thank you for accompanying me on this poetic exploration.